Contents

Making a start

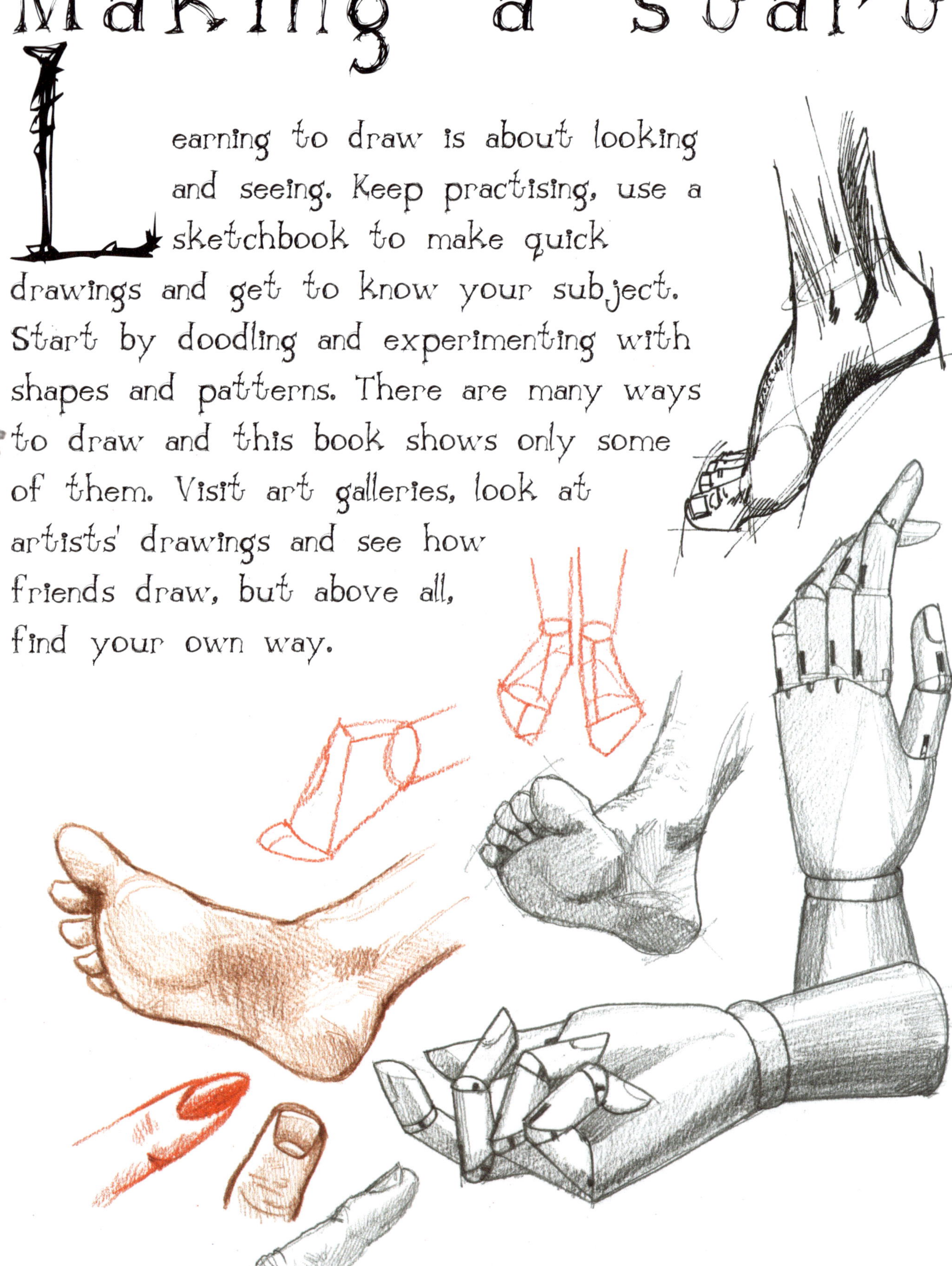

Learning to draw is about looking and seeing. Keep practising, use a sketchbook to make quick drawings and get to know your subject. Start by doodling and experimenting with shapes and patterns. There are many ways to draw and this book shows only some of them. Visit art galleries, look at artists' drawings and see how friends draw, but above all, find your own way.

HOW TO DRAW™
HANDS
AND
FEET

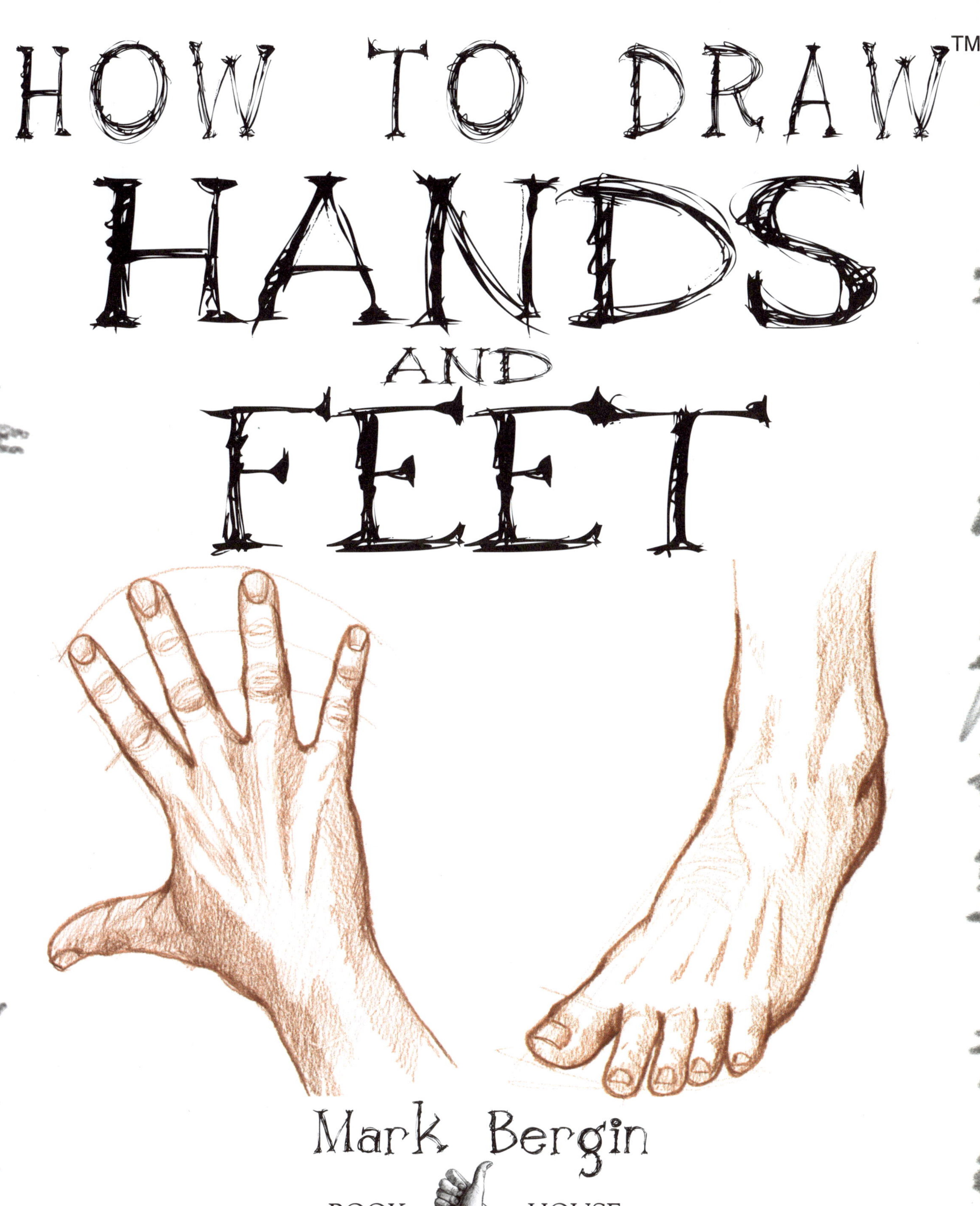

Mark Bergin

BOOK HOUSE

SALARIYA

© The Salariya Book Company Ltd MMXVI
All rights reserved. No part of this book may be reproduced, stored in a retrieval system or transmitted in any form or by any means, electronic, mechanical, photocopying, recording or otherwise, without the written permission of the copyright owner.

Published in Great Britain in MMXVI by
Book House, an imprint of
The Salariya Book Company Ltd
25 Marlborough Place, Brighton BN1 1UB

1 3 5 7 9 8 6 4 2

Author: **Mark Bergin** was born in Hastings in 1961. He studied at Eastbourne College of Art and has specialised in historical reconstructions as well as aviation and maritime subjects since 1983. He lives in Bexhill-on-Sea with his wife and three children.

Editors: Rob Walker, Nick Pierce

PB ISBN: 978-1-910706-17-6

A CIP catalogue record for this book is available from the British Library.

Printed and bound in China.
Printed on paper from sustainable sources.

WARNING: Fixatives should be used only under adult supervision.

Visit our websites to read interactive **free** web books, stay up to date with new releases, catch up with us on the Book House Blog, view our electronic catalogue and more!

www.salariya.com
Free electronic versions of four of our *You Wouldn't Want to Be* titles

www.book-house.co.uk
Online catalogue
Information books and graphic novels

www.scribobooks.com
Fiction books

www.scribblersbooks.com
Books for babies, toddlers and pre-school children

www.flickr.com/photos/ salariyabookhouse
View our photostream with sneak previews of forthcoming titles

Join the conversation on Facebook and Twitter by visiting
www.salariya.com

Visit our YouTube channel to see Mark Bergin doing step-by-step illustrations:
www.youtube.com/user/ theSalariya

Visit
www.salariya.com
for our online catalogue and **free** interactive web books.

Sketch pads: You can always find a
hand model – use your own hand!

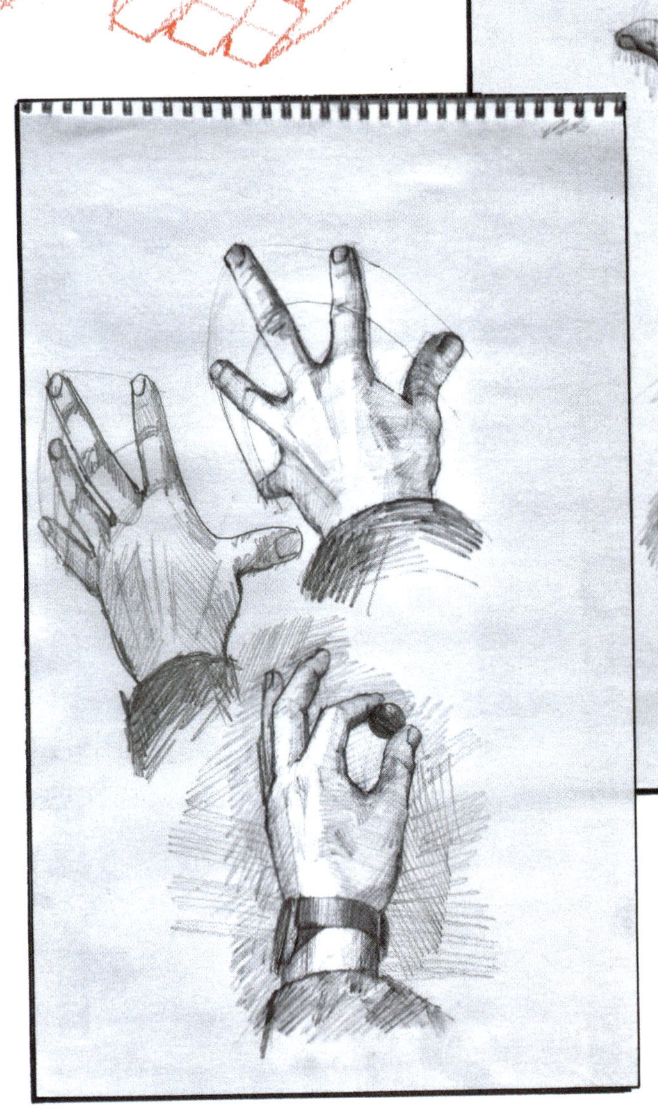

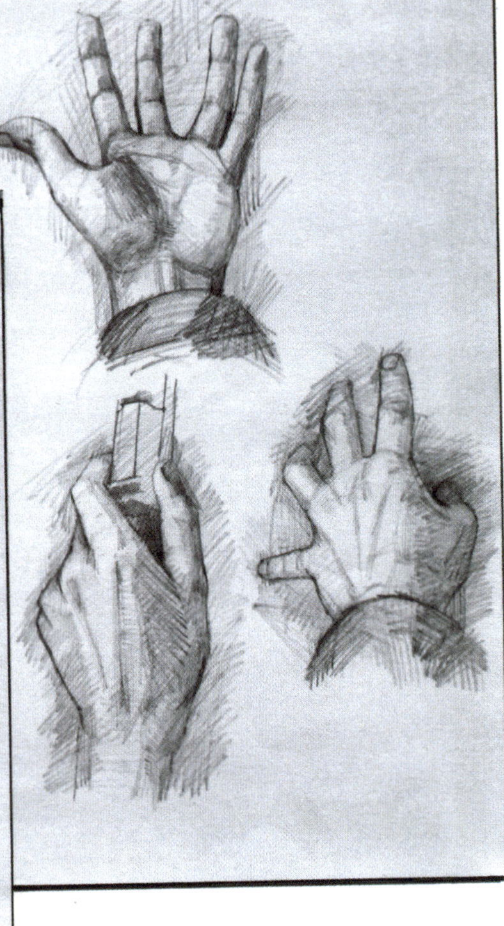

Materials

First, you need to decide what medium you want to use. Try different types of drawing papers and materials. Experiment with charcoal, wax crayons and pastels. All pens, from felt-tips to ballpoints, will make interesting marks. Try drawing with pen and ink on wet paper.

Adding light and shade to a drawing with an ink pen can be tricky. Use solid ink for the very darkest areas and cross-hatching (straight lines criss-crossing each other) for ordinary dark tones. Use hatching (straight lines running parallel to each other) for midtones, and leave the white of the paper for the lightest areas.

Graphic ink pen

Crayons

Crayons come in a wide range of colours. They are incredibly soft and are easily smudged. Use fixative to protect the drawing.

Ink silhouette

Silhouette is a style of drawing that shows only a solid black shape, like a shadow.

Brush pens allow for the same versatility as a paint brush, letting you draw pictures with very fine or very strong lines.

Brush Pens

Pencil drawings can include a vast amount of detail and tone. Try experimenting with different grades of pencil to get a range of light and shade effects in your drawing.

Remember, the best equipment and materials will not necessarily make the best drawing — only practice will!

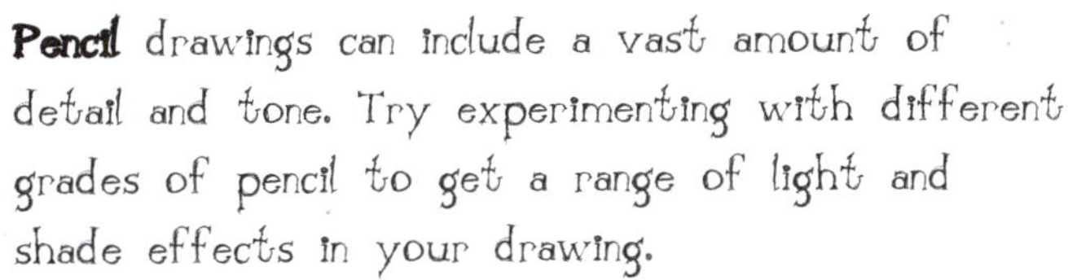

HB Pencil

Inside the hands

The structure of the human hand is highly complex. It has 27 bones, including the eight short bones in the carpus (or wrist), and the phalanges (or finger bones). To be able to draw a hand accurately, you should find out about the underlying muscular and skeletal structure that create its shape and the complexity of its movement.

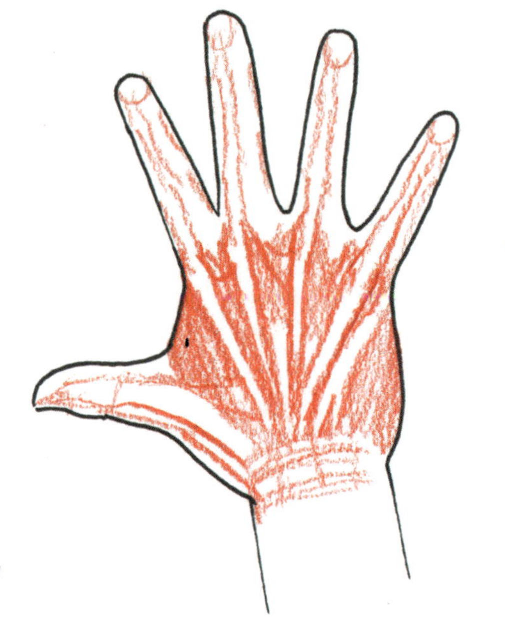

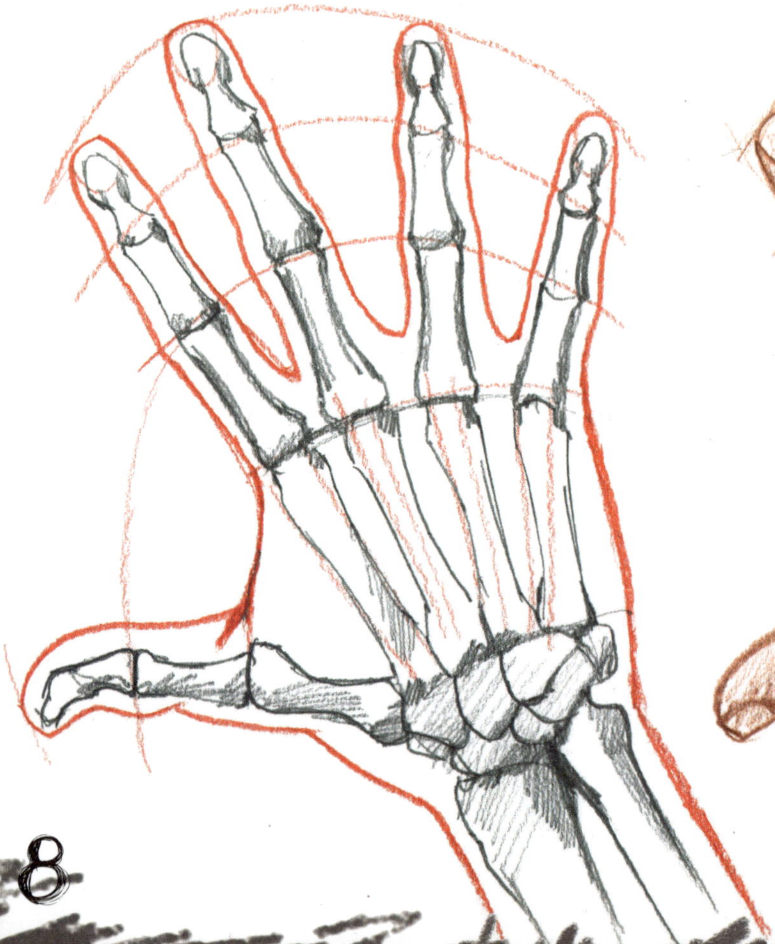

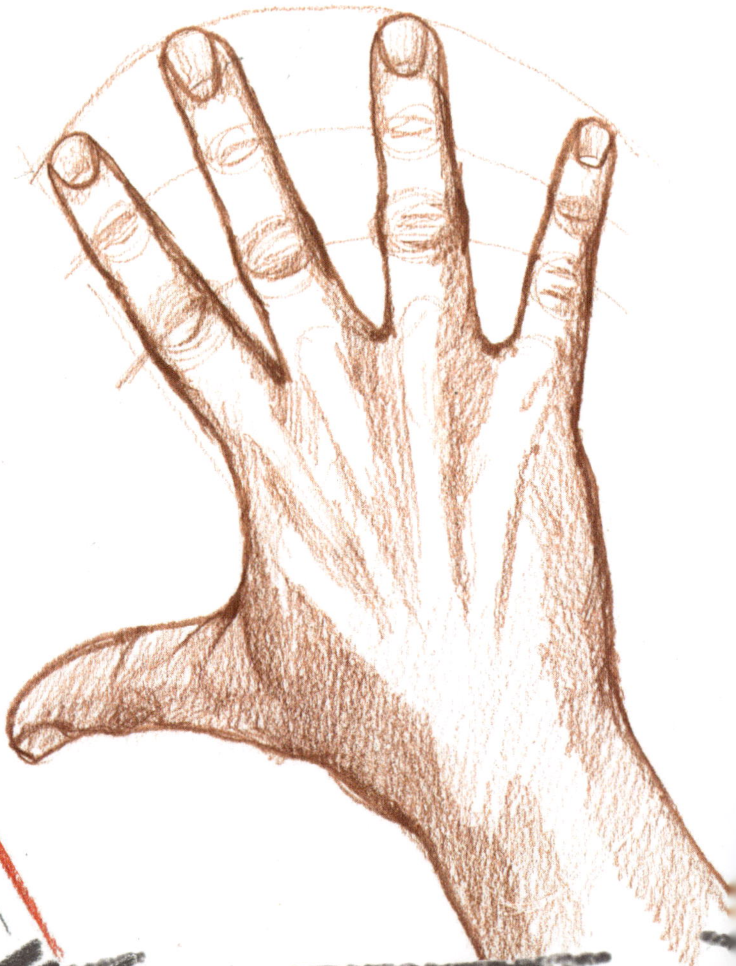

Main ligaments and muscles on
the surface of the hand (left)
and palm (right).

Bone structure of hand

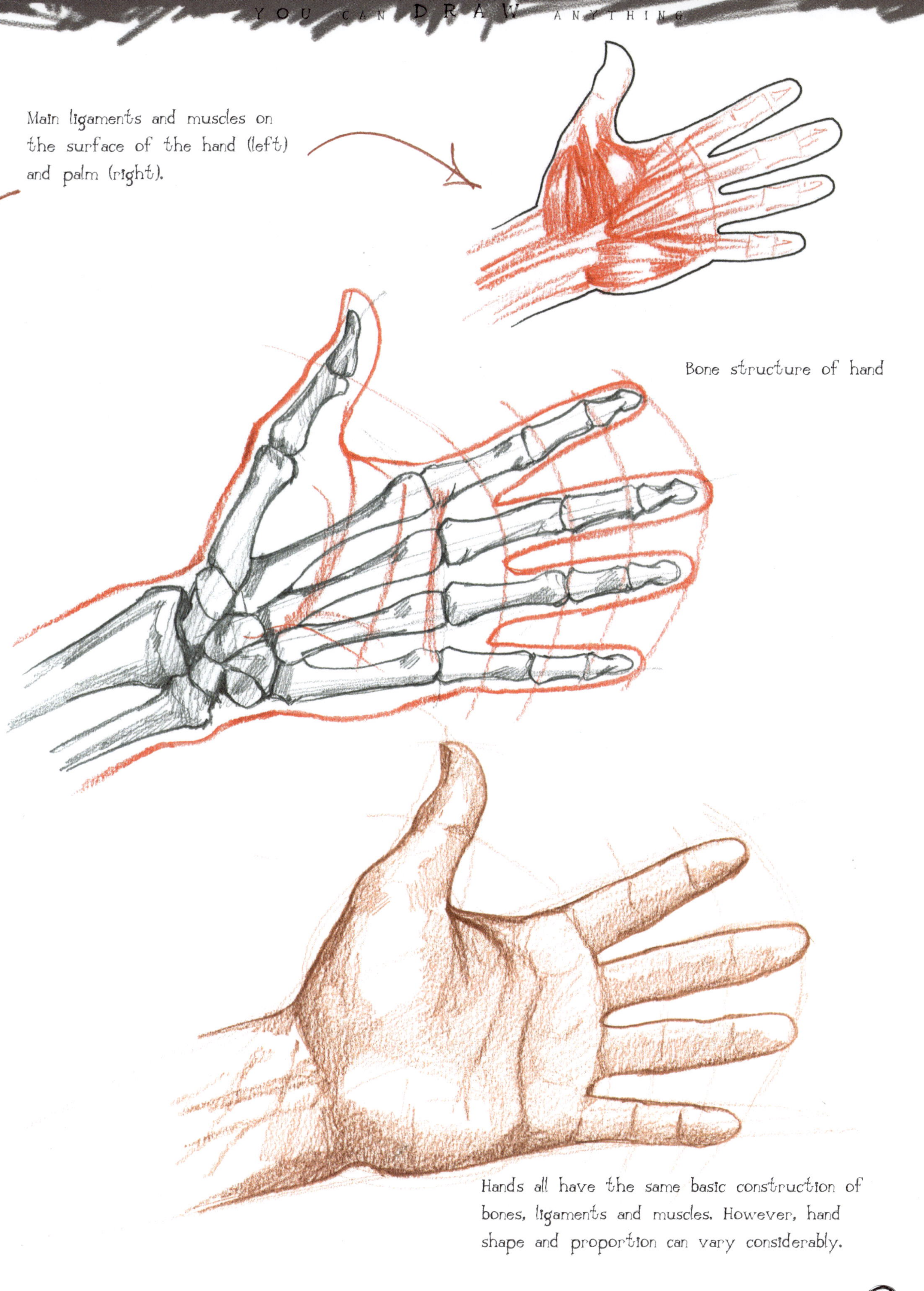

Hands all have the same basic construction of
bones, ligaments and muscles. However, hand
shape and proportion can vary considerably.

Basic construction of hands

Doing lots of quick sketches will strengthen your understanding of the shapes and proportions of hands. This will give your drawings a much greater sense of solidity and accuracy of construction.

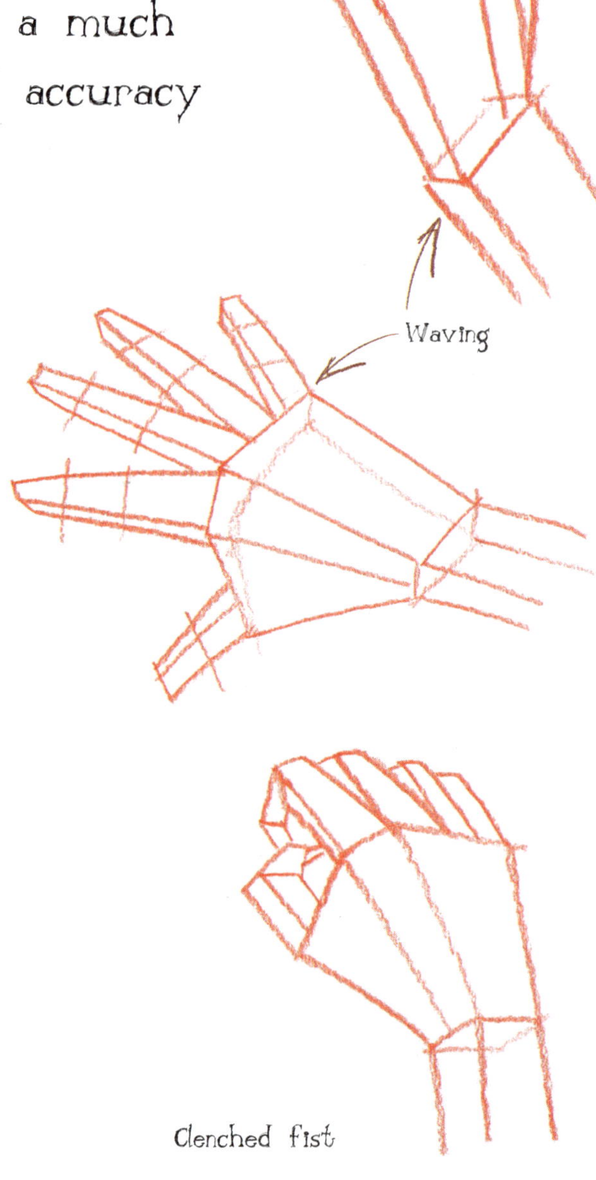

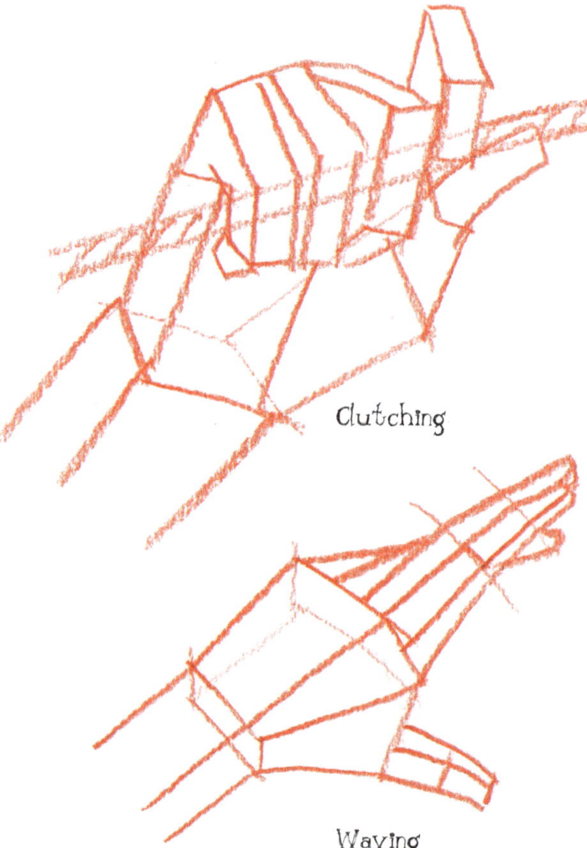

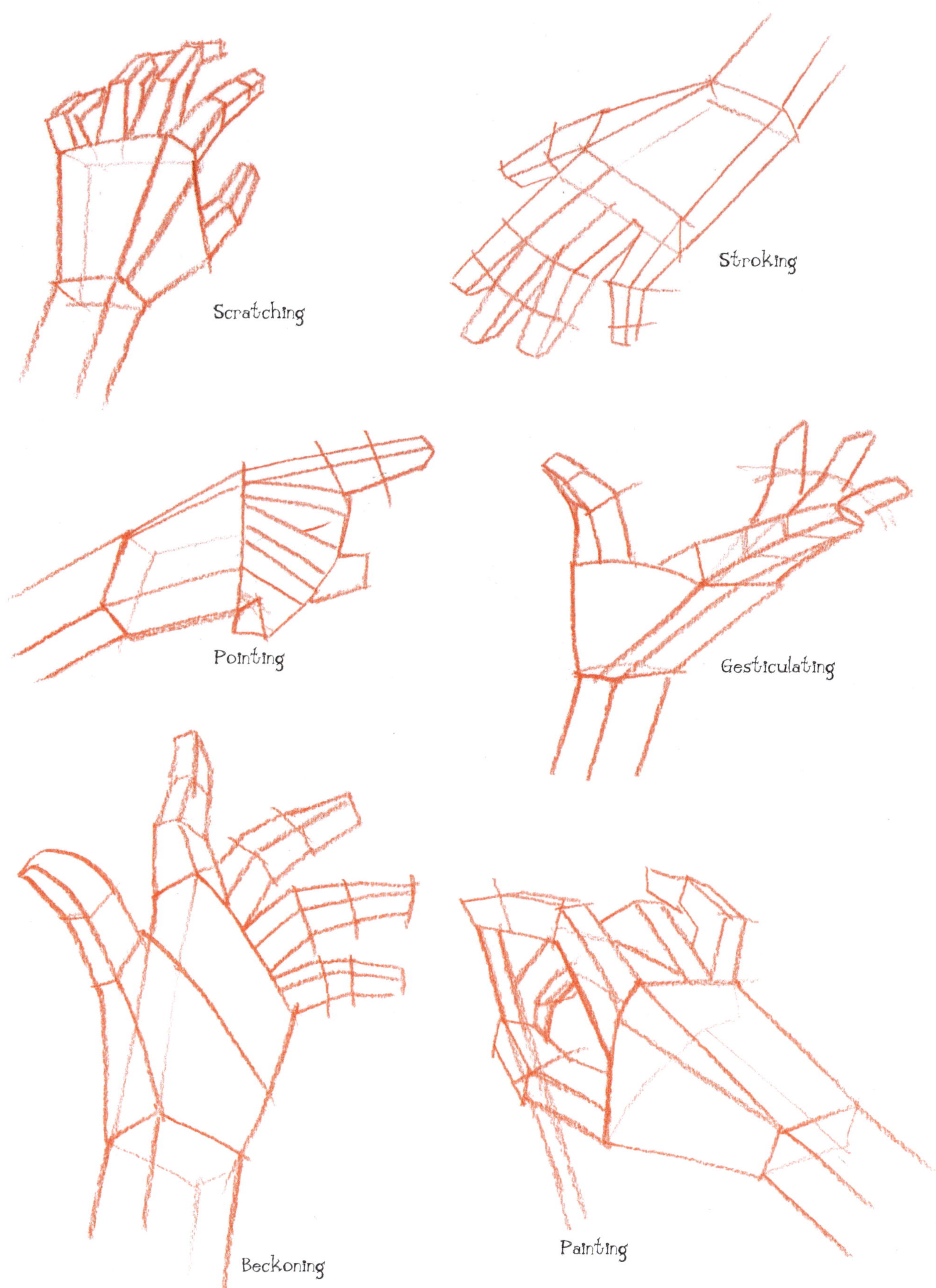

Scratching
Stroking
Pointing
Gesticulating
Beckoning
Painting

Dynamic hands

Human hands are highly developed and capable of performing very complicated and intricate actions. When humans evolved opposable thumbs we were able to grip and manipulate things more easily than other creatures. This is why the thumb is often called "the master digit".

Gesture

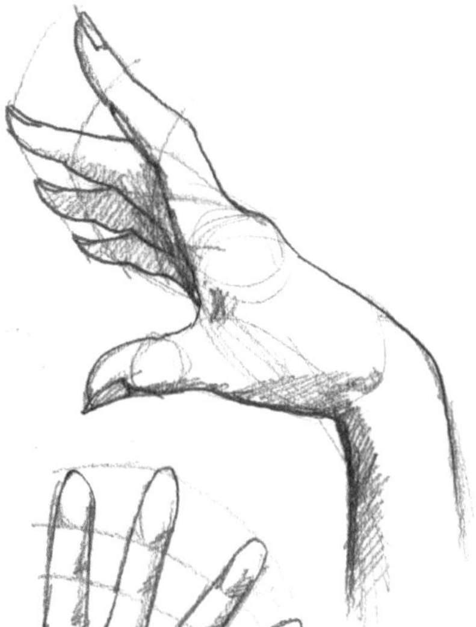

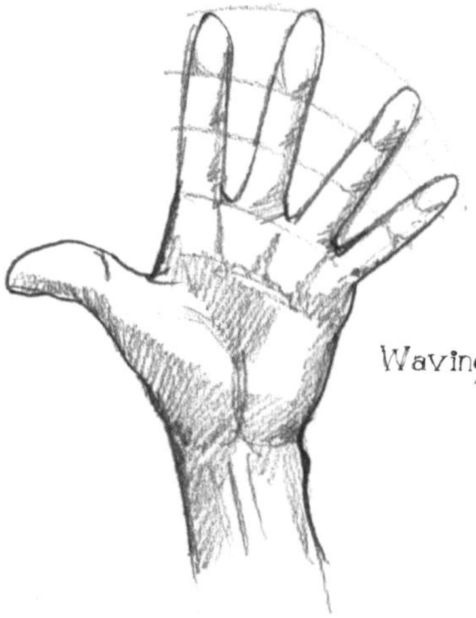

Waving

Praying

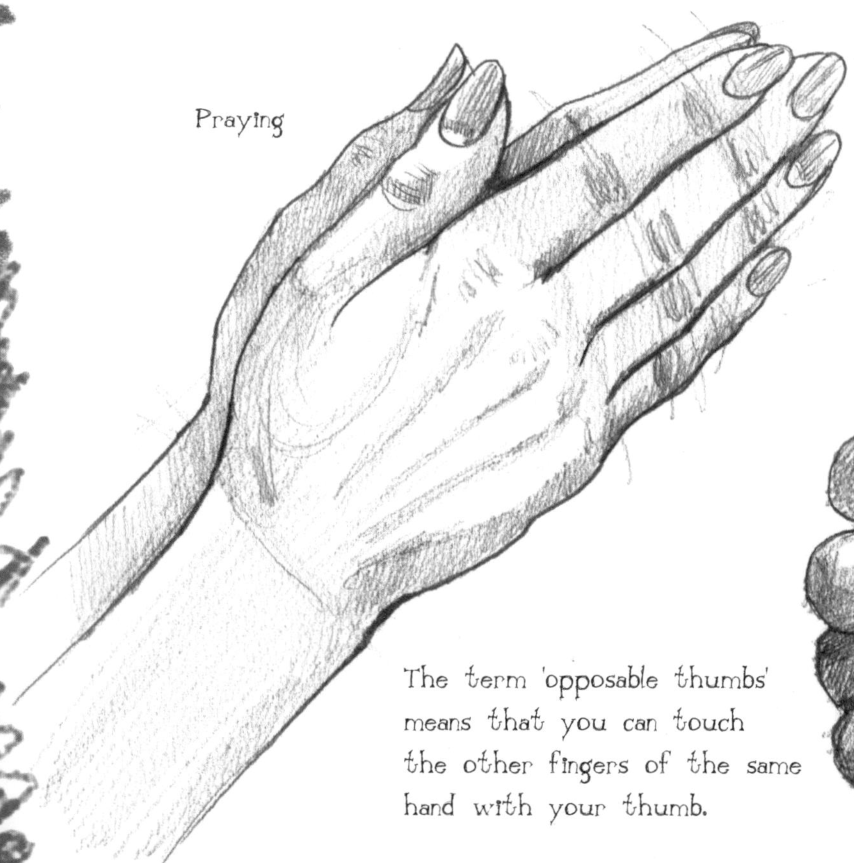

Thumbs up

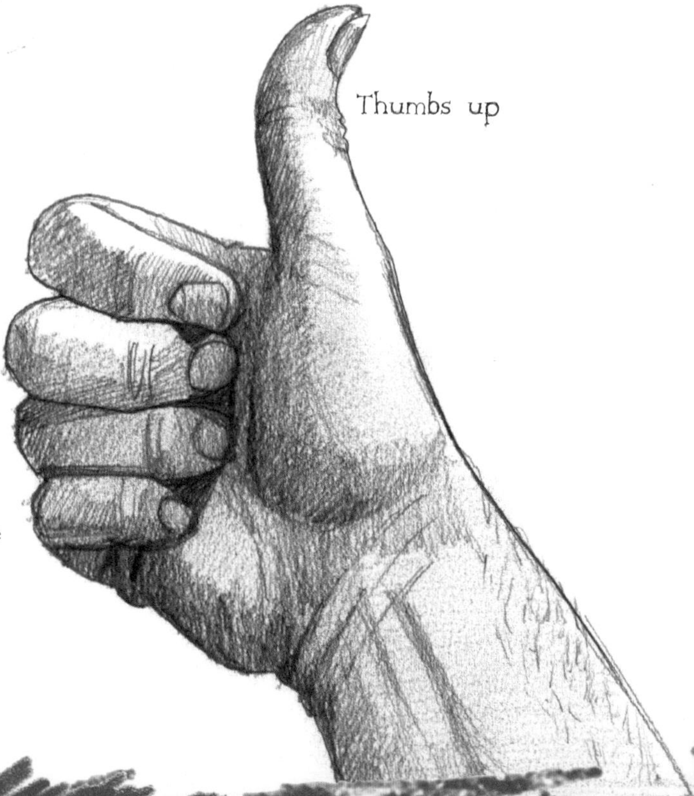

The term 'opposable thumbs' means that you can touch the other fingers of the same hand with your thumb.

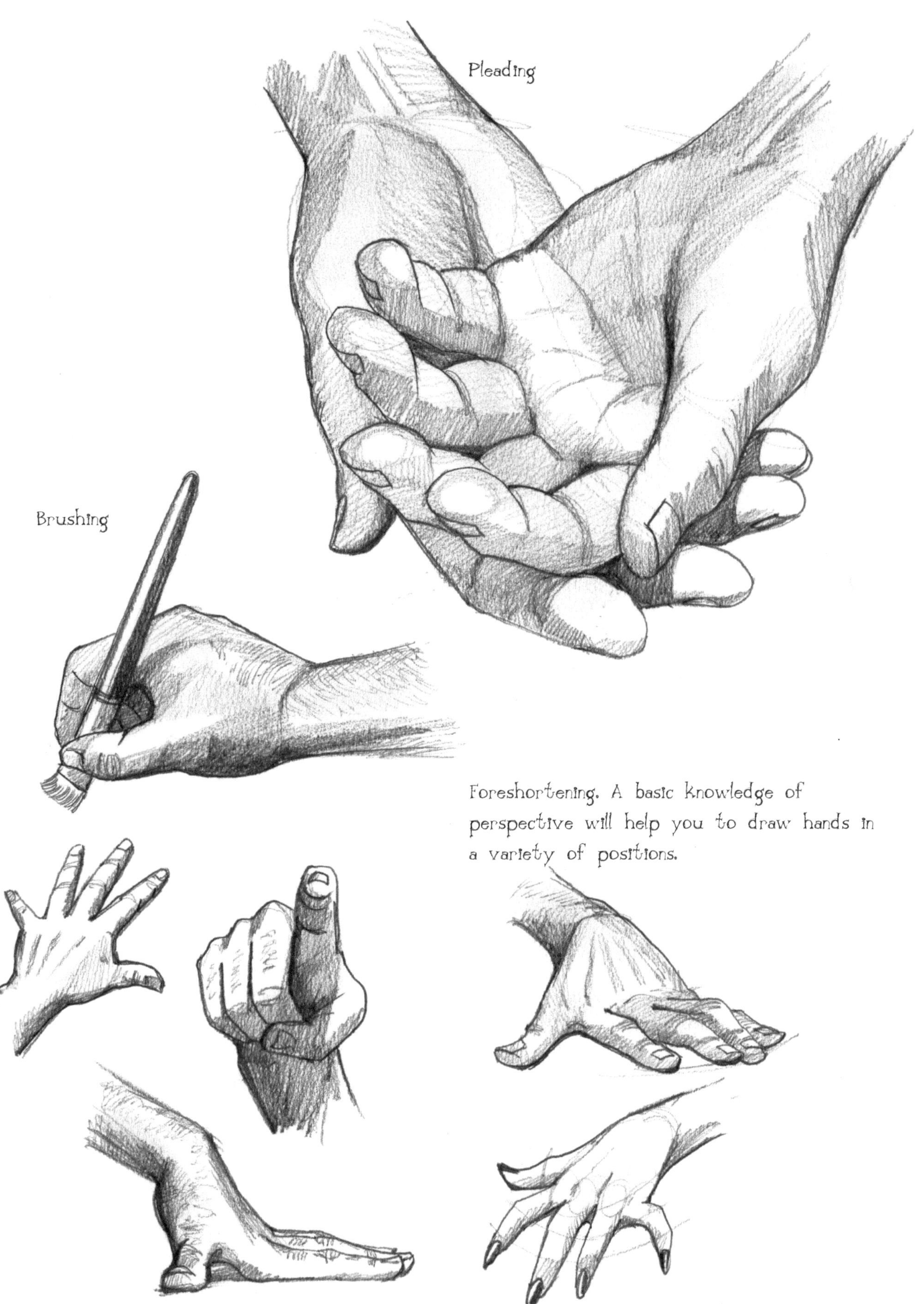

Pleading

Brushing

Foreshortening. A basic knowledge of
perspective will help you to draw hands in
a variety of positions.

Different hand sizes

The average length of an adult male hand from wrist to fingertip is 189mm. A woman's hand is around 172 mm long. This difference in size between male and female hands is part of what is called sexual dimorphism. To make your drawings representative you need to show the variations in size and shape of the hands of a man, a woman or a child.

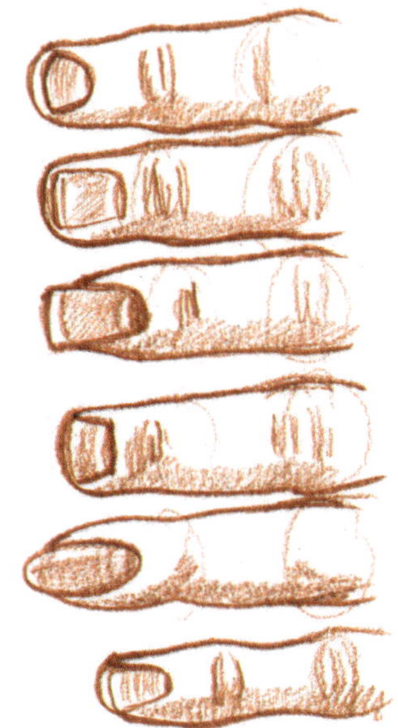

Variations of nail and finger shapes (round, square and oval)

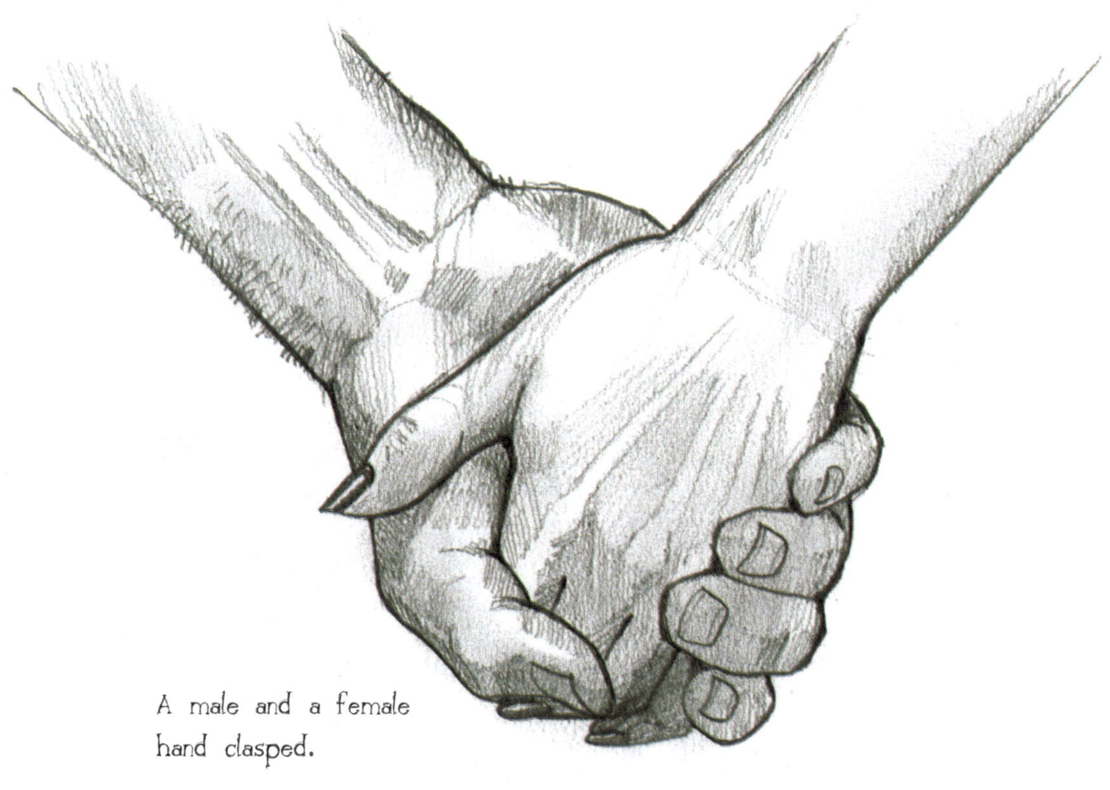

A male and a female hand clasped.

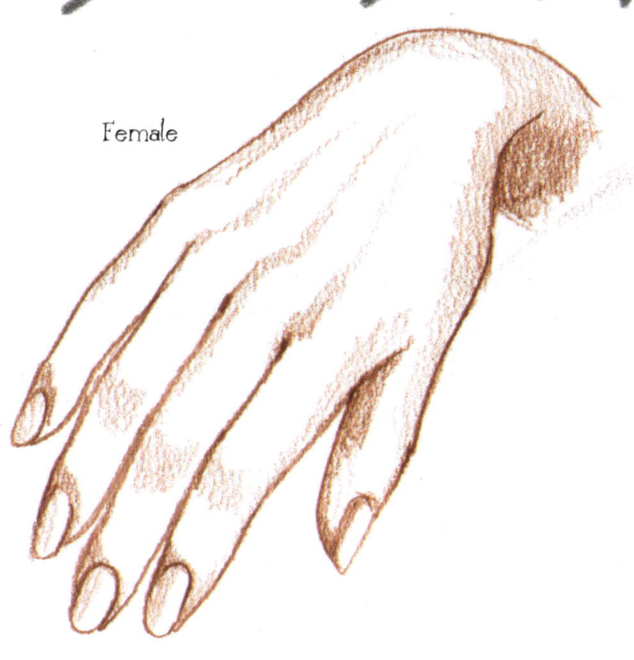

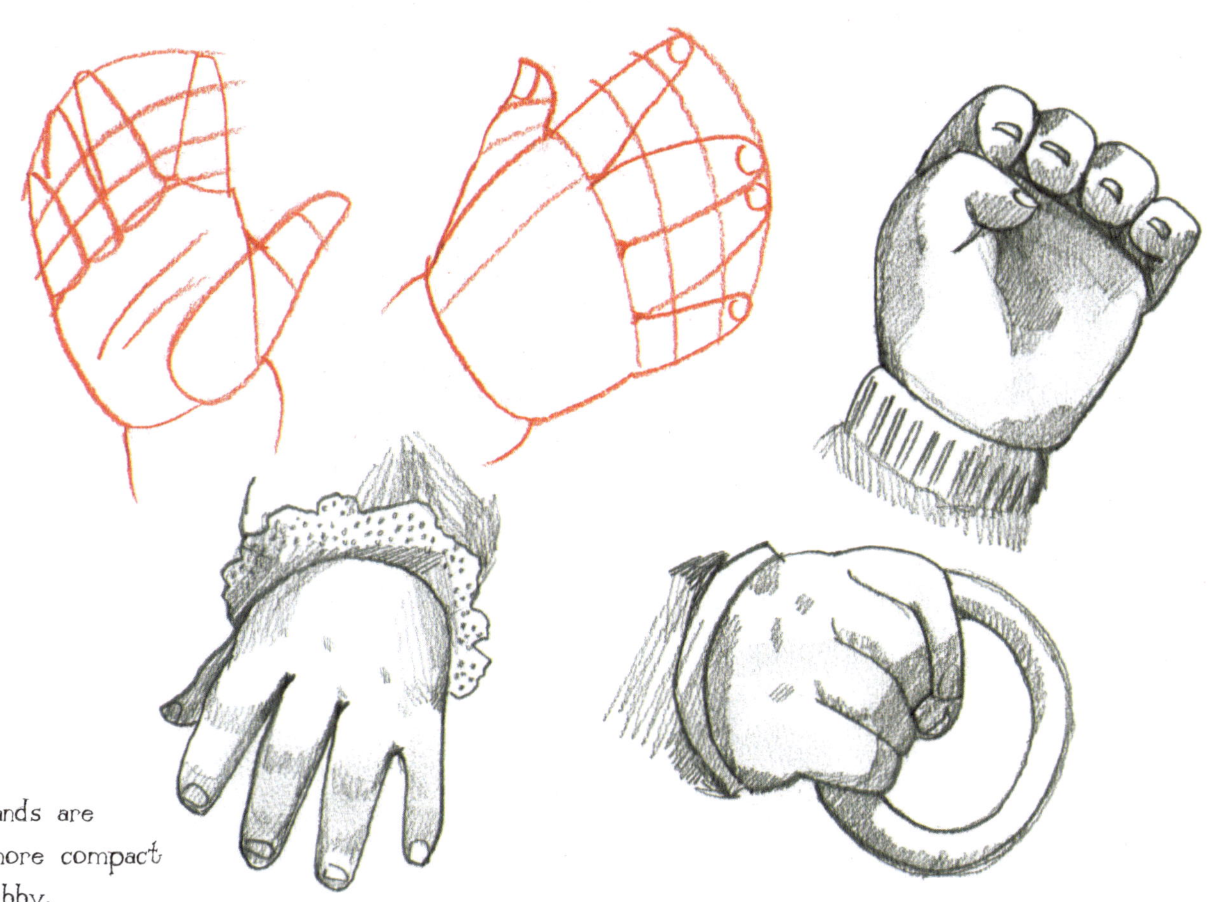

Baby hands are much more compact and chubby.

Hands and character

Hands can reveal a lot about a person's lifestyle, such as the effects of outdoor work or manual labour. Hands become wrinkled in old age partly because the body produces less collagen and oil. Environmental factors like exposure to sunlight or smoking also contribute.

Look at the space around the drawing (**negative space**) to help check the proportions and shape of your drawing.

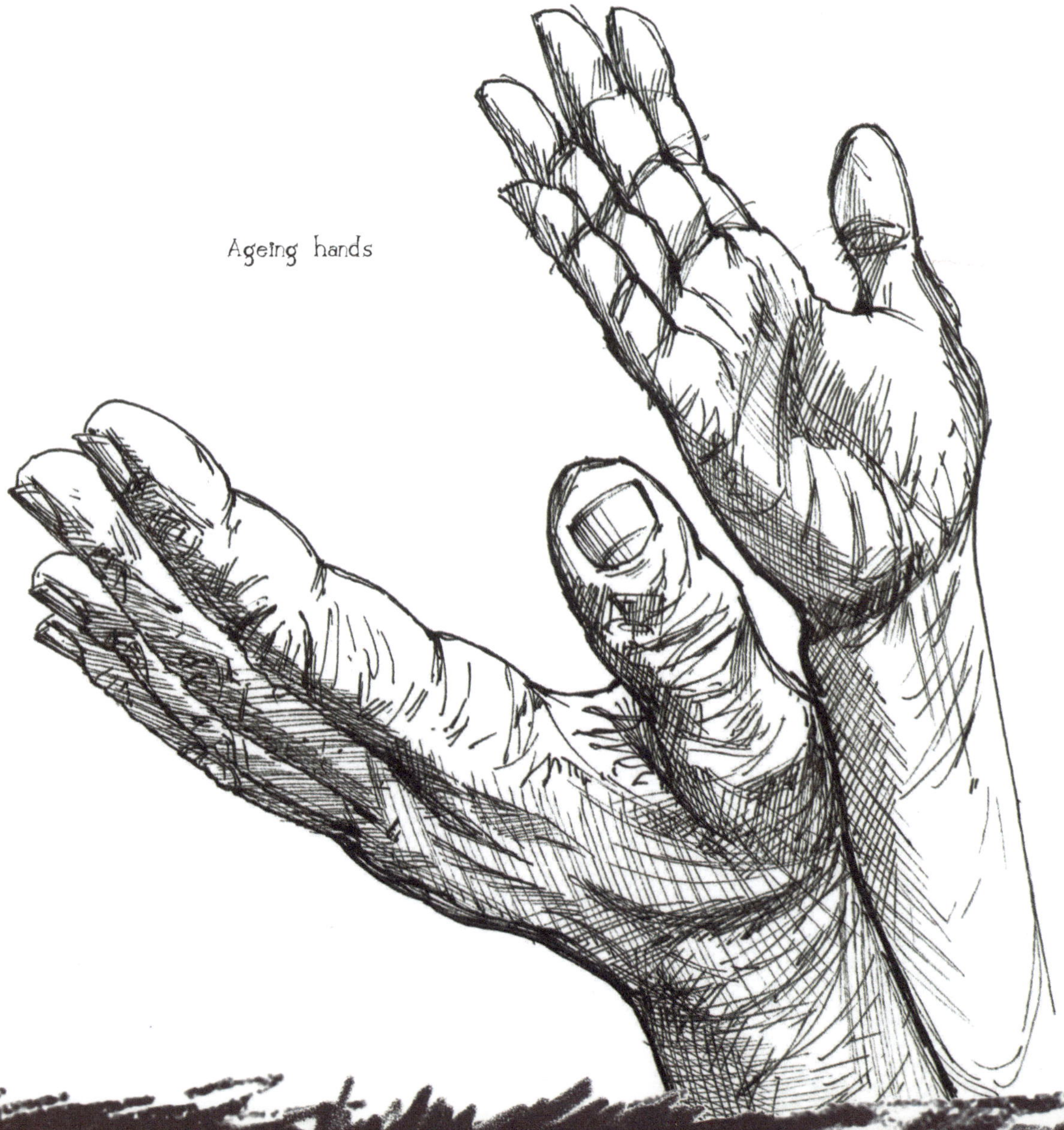

Ageing hands

Look for features and marks that distinguish
the hand like tendons, prominent veins, and hair,
spots and creases.

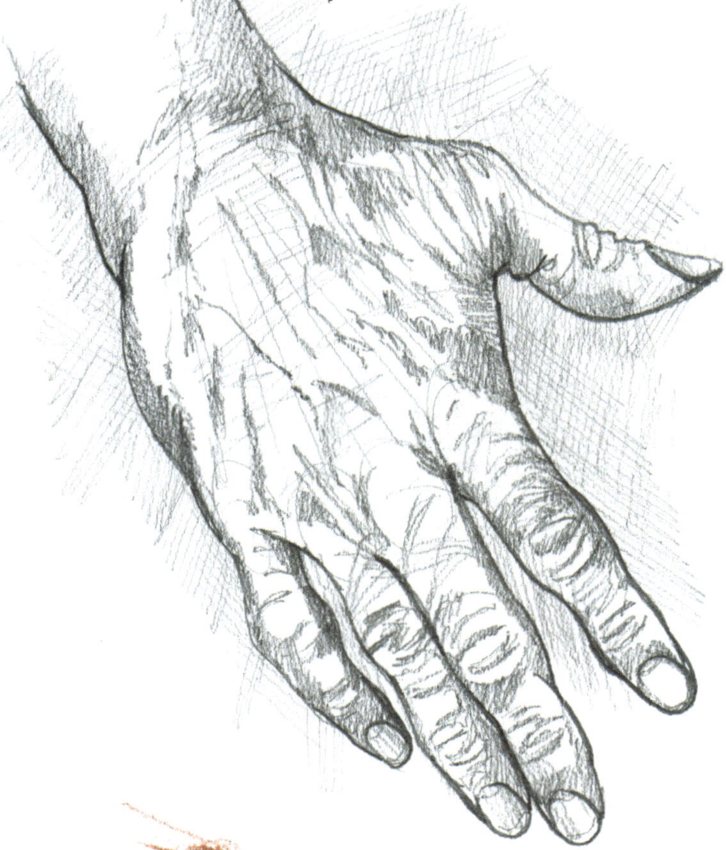

Gloved hands

Gloves are worn for comfort and protection from the outside world. In sport and manual labour, they help to prevent injury. In cold weather gloves keep your hands warm and flexible and prevent your skin from drying. Gloves are made for many different purposes and come in many shapes that can add great interest to a drawing.

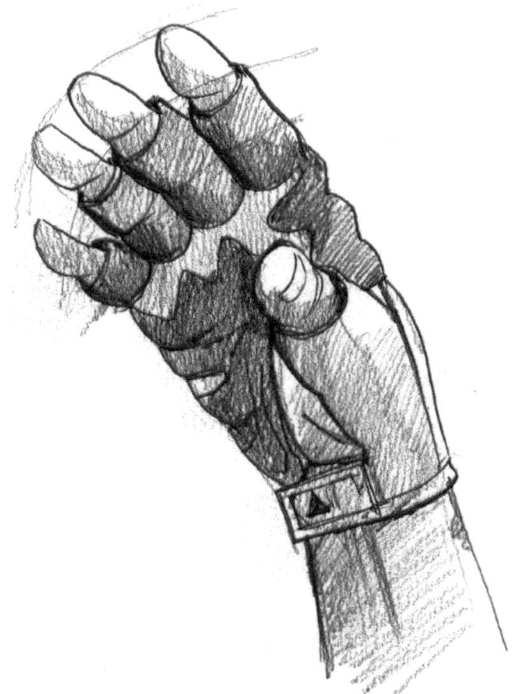

Golf glove

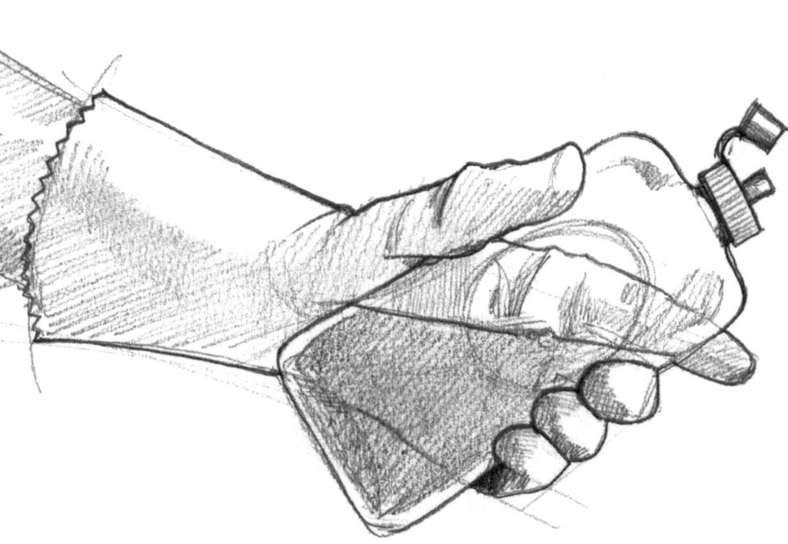

Rubber washing-up glove

Sailing glove

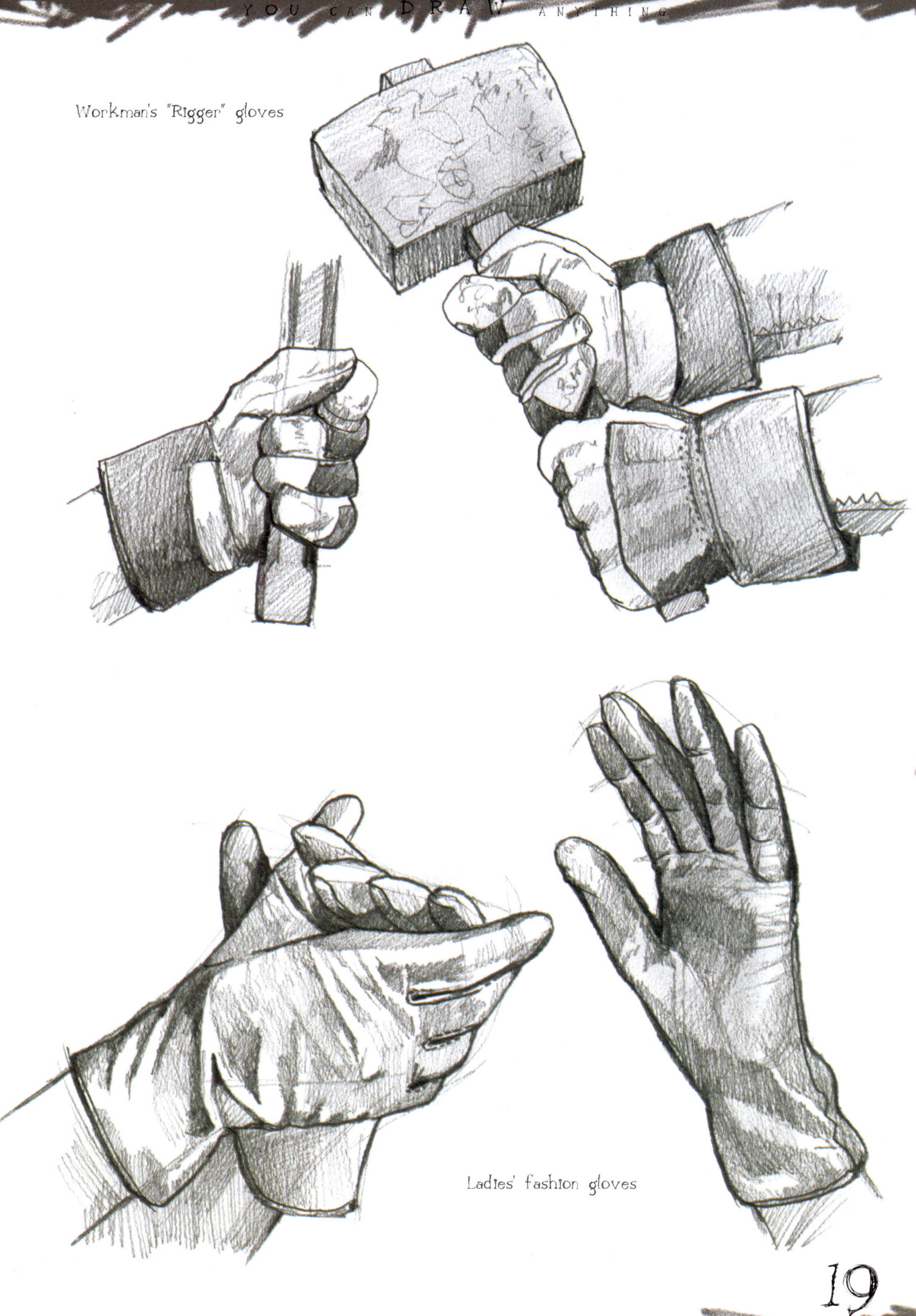

Workman's "Rigger" gloves
Ladies' fashion gloves

Light and shade

Drawing hands can be difficult. Careful observation of the direction and strength of the light source can help you to define their form. Then you can use shading to add texture and shadows to your drawings.

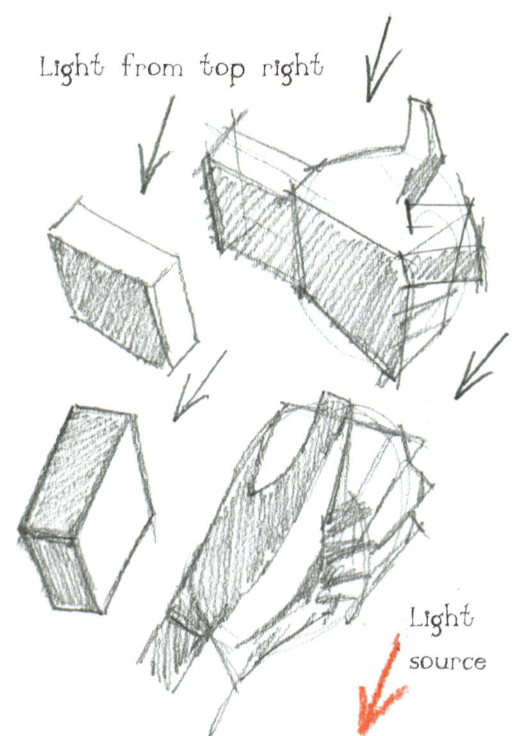

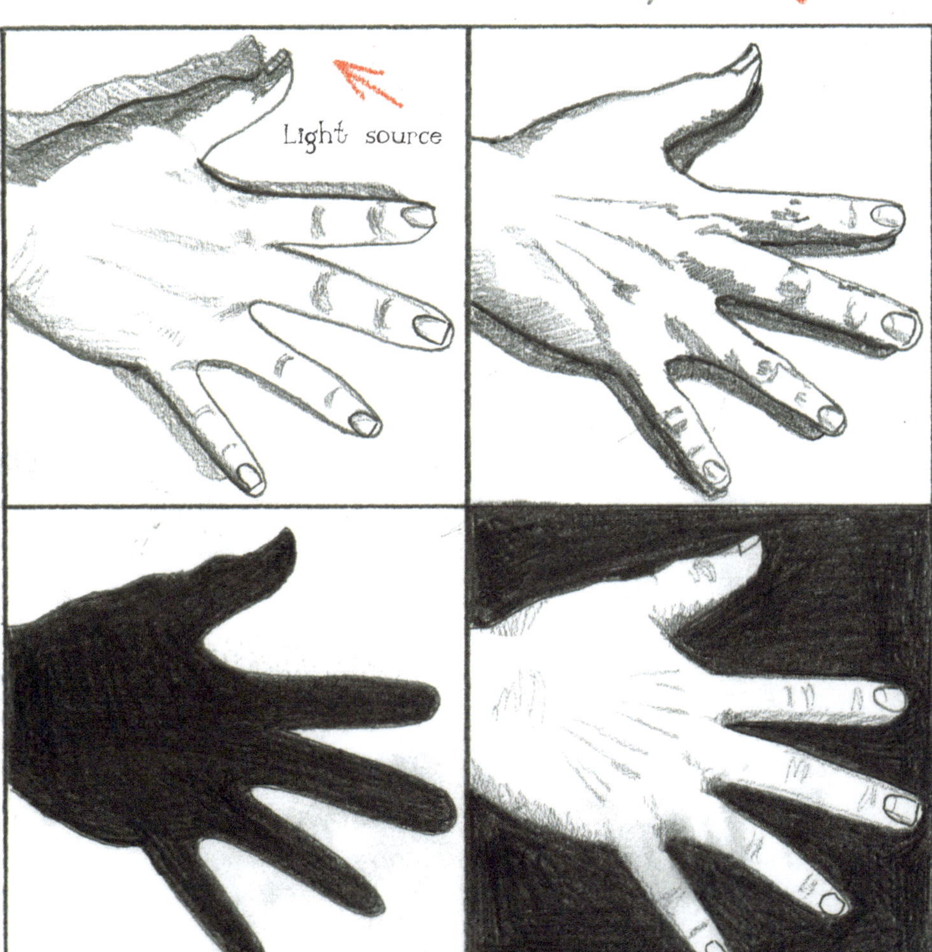

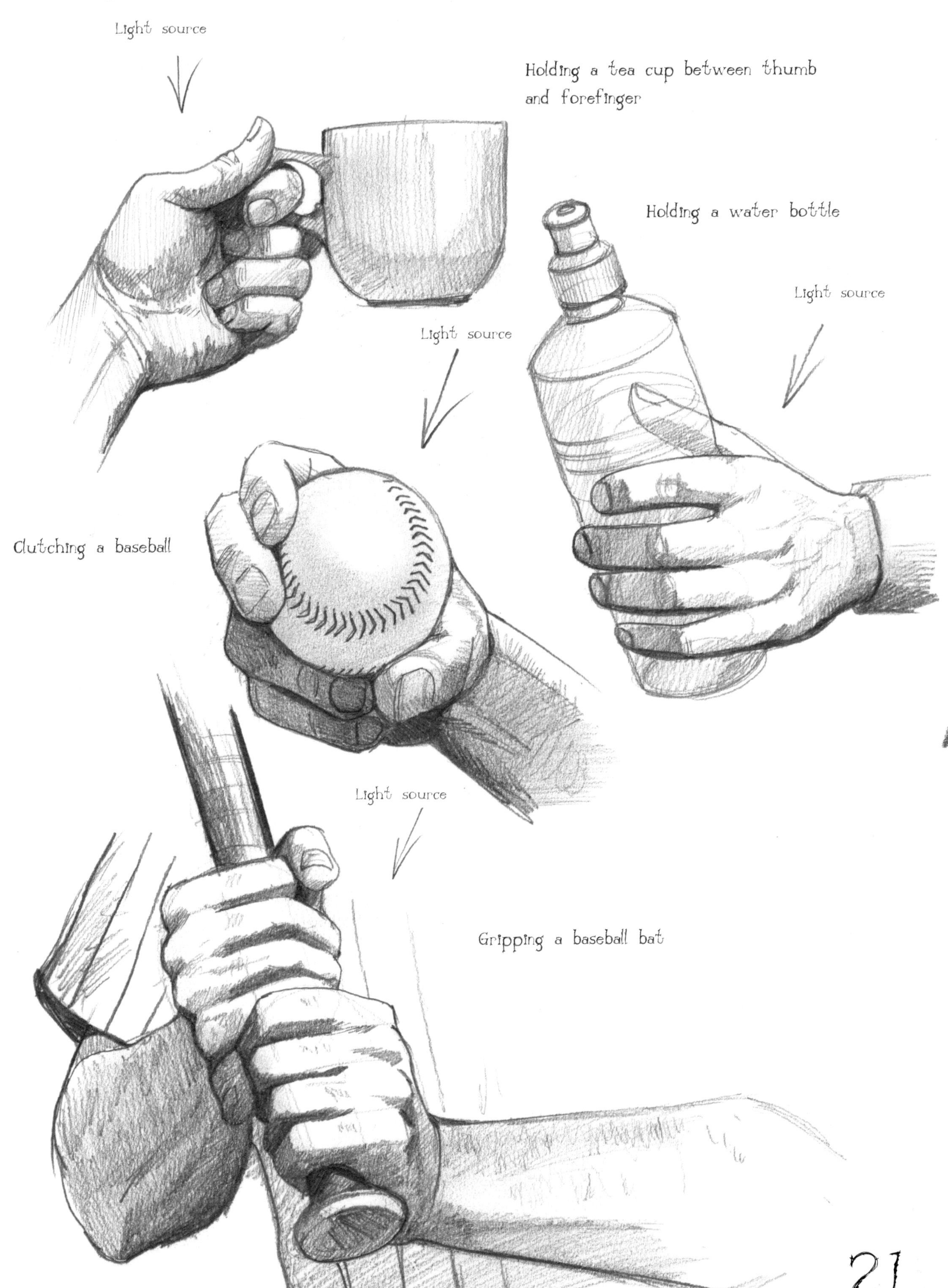
Light source
Holding a tea cup between thumb and forefinger
Holding a water bottle
Light source
Light source
Clutching a baseball
Light source
Gripping a baseball bat

Two handed actions

One hand can perform very complicated actions by itself, but two hands working together can carry out even more amazing feats! Without the interaction of both your hands and their ten digits, you wouldn't be able to play an instrument, knit a jumper or drive a car.

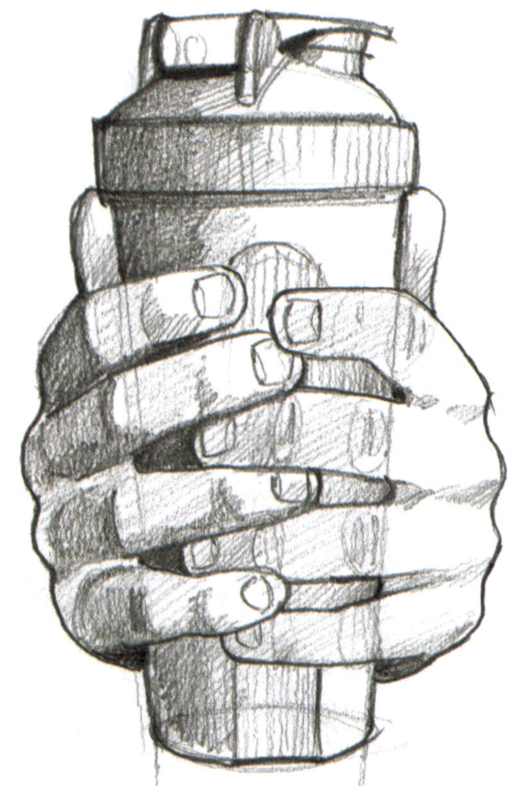

Holding a thermos

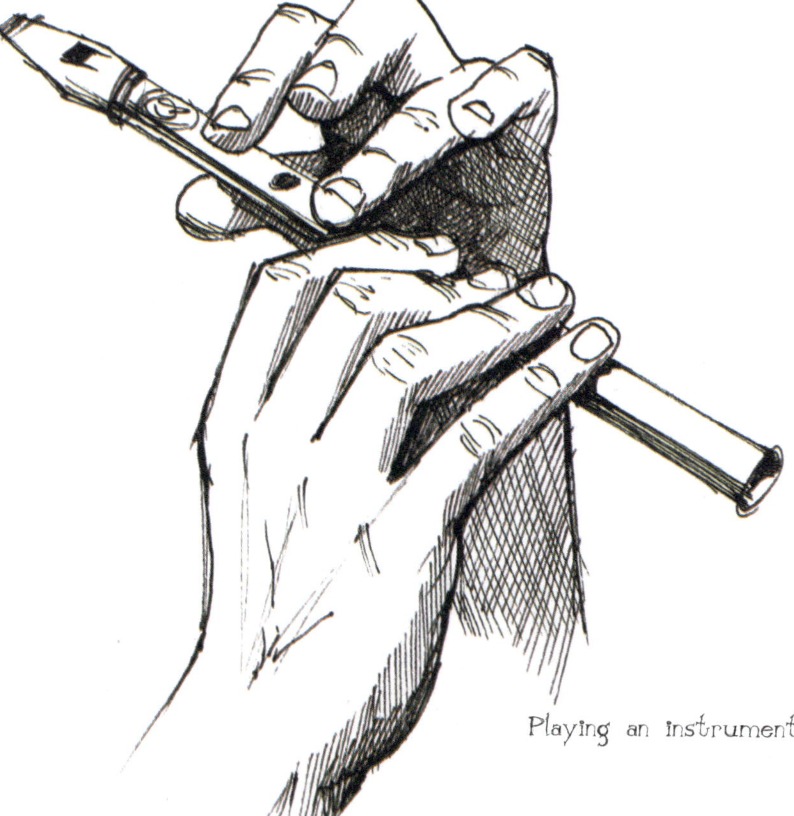

Playing an instrument

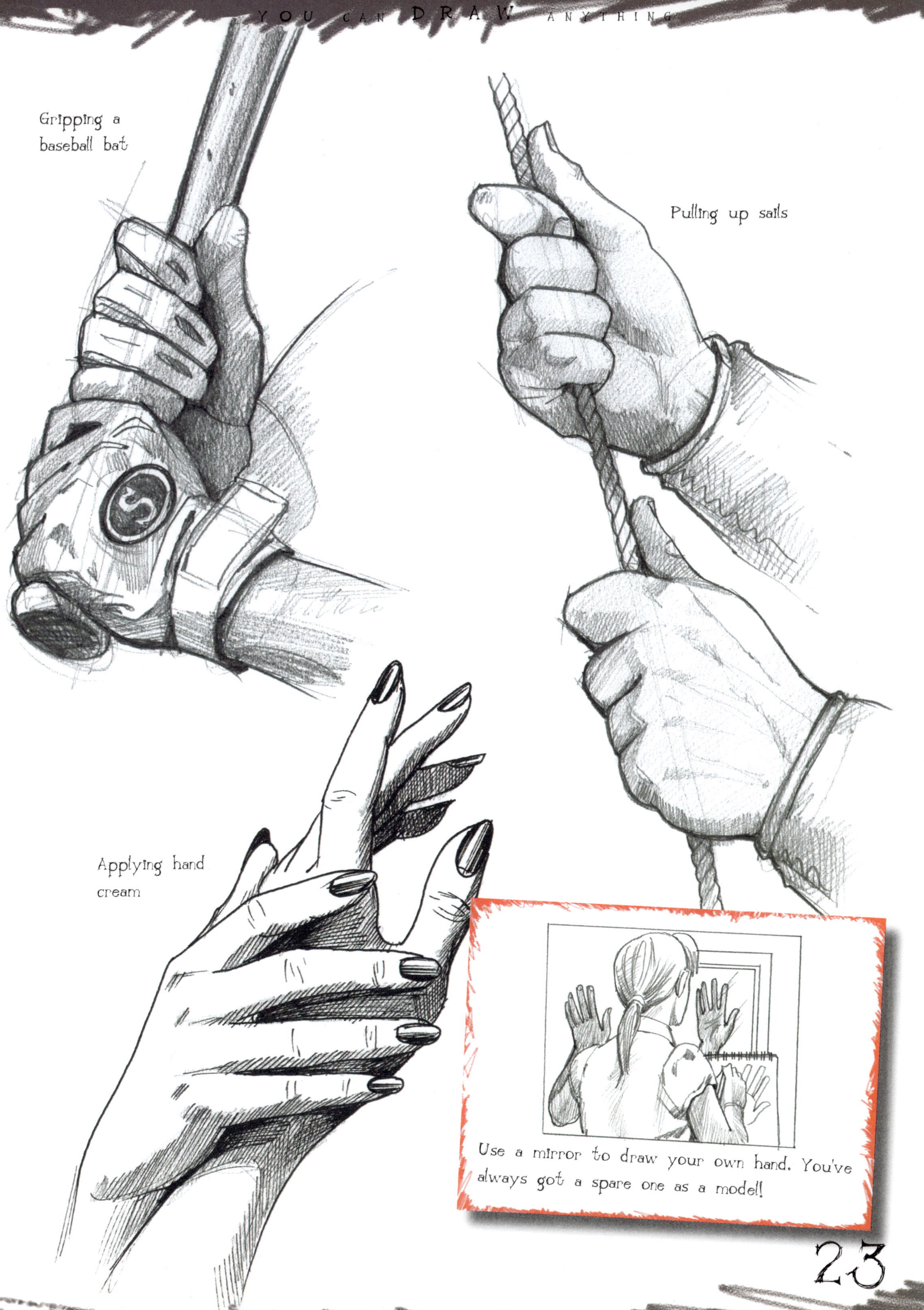

Gripping a
baseball bat

Pulling up sails

Applying hand
cream

Use a mirror to draw your own hand. You've
always got a spare one as a model!

Inside the feet

The human foot is just as complex a structure as the hand. It contains 26 bones, 33 joints and more than a hundred ligaments, tendons and muscles. Over a quarter of all the bones in the human body are in your feet. In an average person's lifetime, they will walk 115,000 miles, or more than four times around the world.

Skeleton

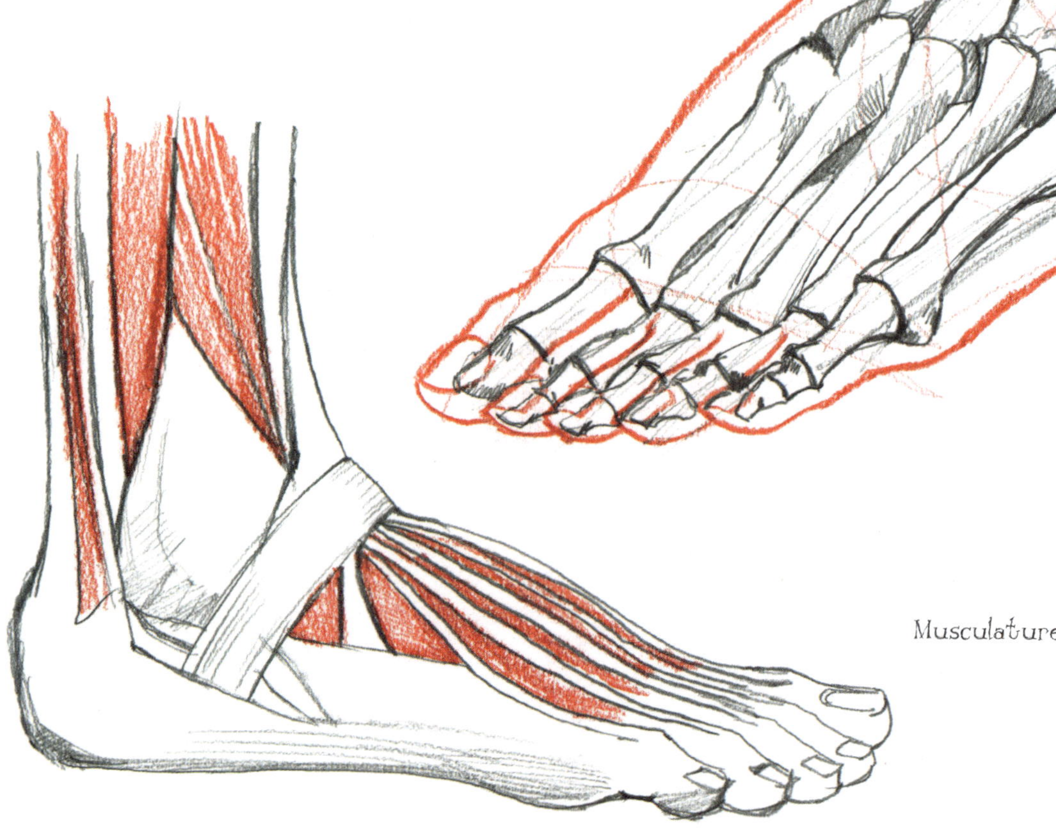

Musculature

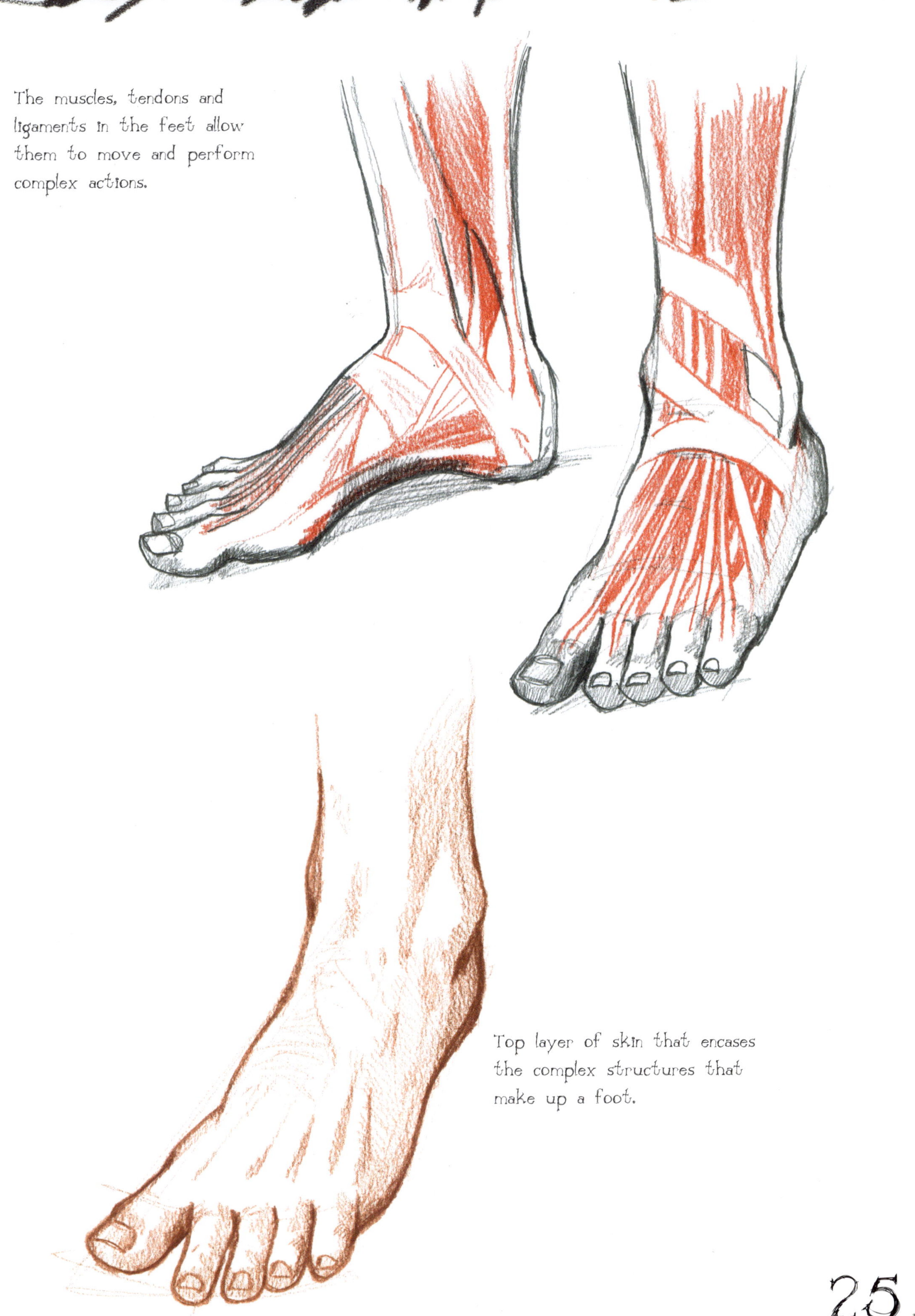

The muscles, tendons and ligaments in the feet allow them to move and perform complex actions.

Top layer of skin that encases the complex structures that make up a foot.

Basic construction of feet

Use simple shapes such as circles, rectangles and squares to sketch the initial construction of a foot. Take care to get the proportions and perspective right before you start adding more detail.

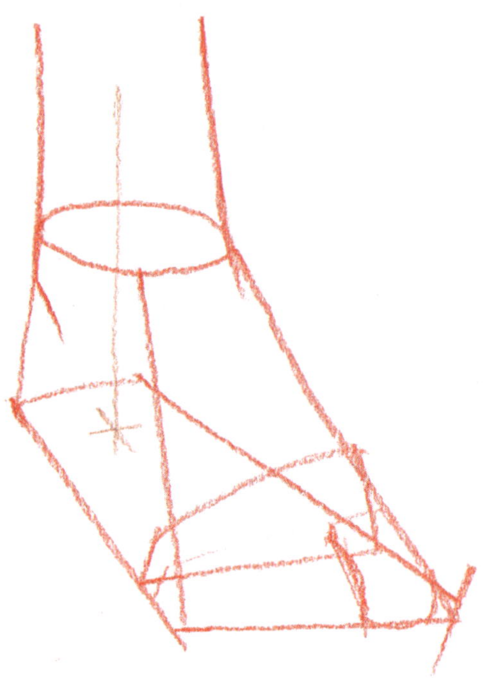

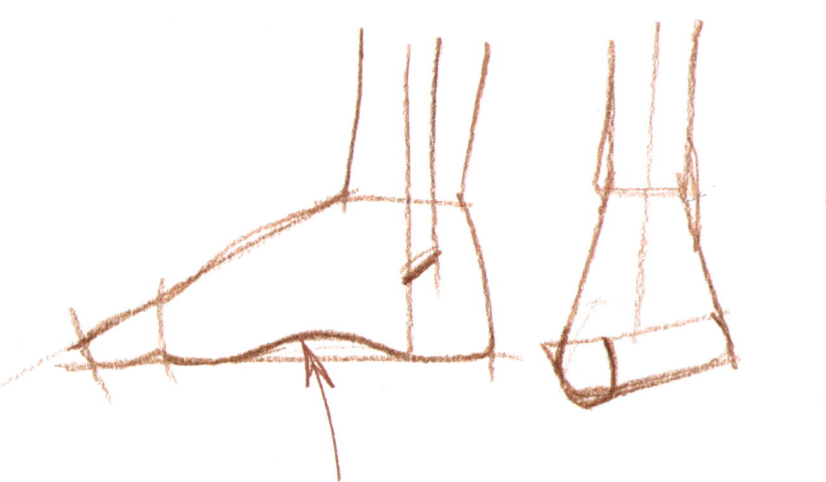

The inside edge reveals the foot arch.

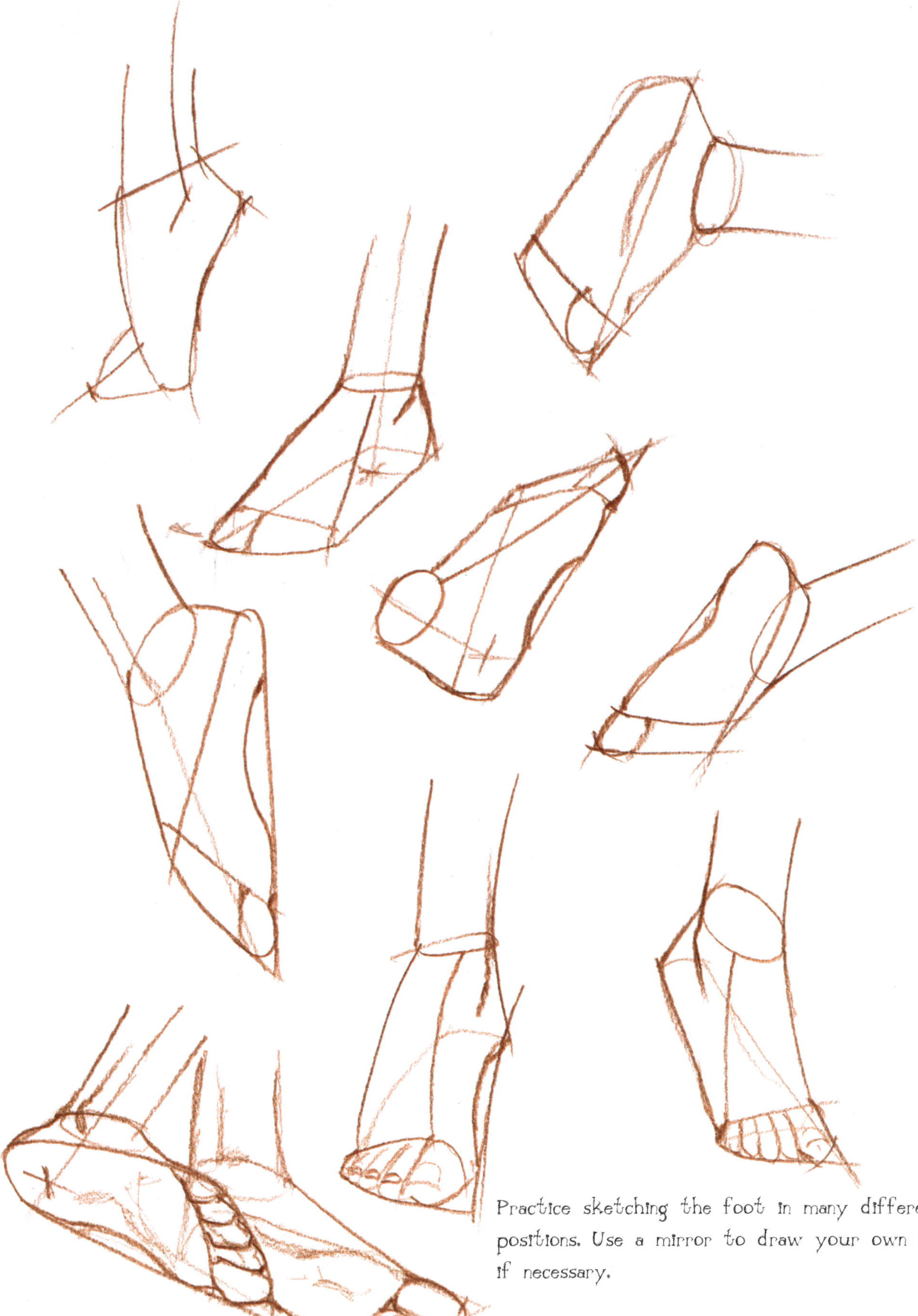

Practice sketching the foot in many different positions. Use a mirror to draw your own foot if necessary.

Feet working together

Just like your hands, two feet working together can create endless possibilities. Thanks to the coordination and strength of your feet, you can dance, run a marathon or score a hat trick. When drawing both feet together look at the spaces and angles between them. This will tell you a great deal about the motion, position and weight of the body they support.

Ballet dancer's feet
(capable of extreme poses)

Feet can express emotion, personality and posture.

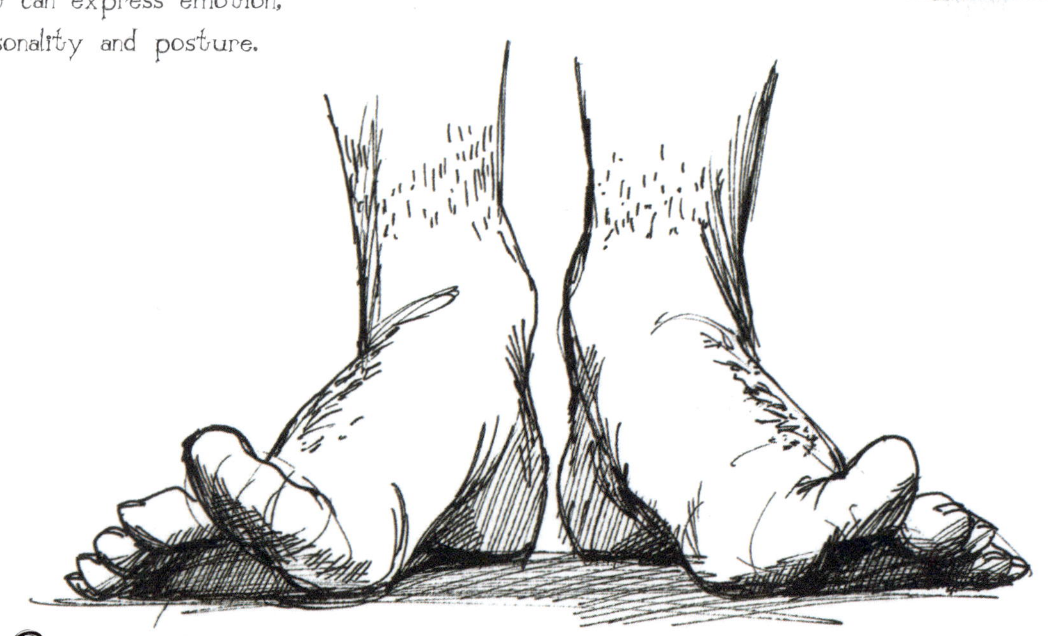

Dancing feet

Synchronised swimmer's feet

Runner's feet

Baby feet
(chubby and less sure-footed)

Light and shade

To make your drawing more realistic, it is important to capture accurately how light falls across the feet. Experiment with a variety of light sources coming from different directions. A stronger light source will help to define shape and form.

Practice drawing feet in many positions and different light sources.

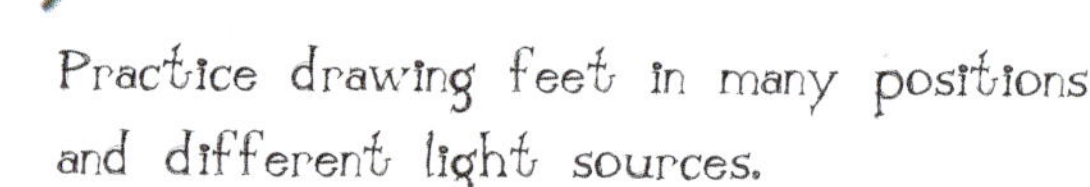

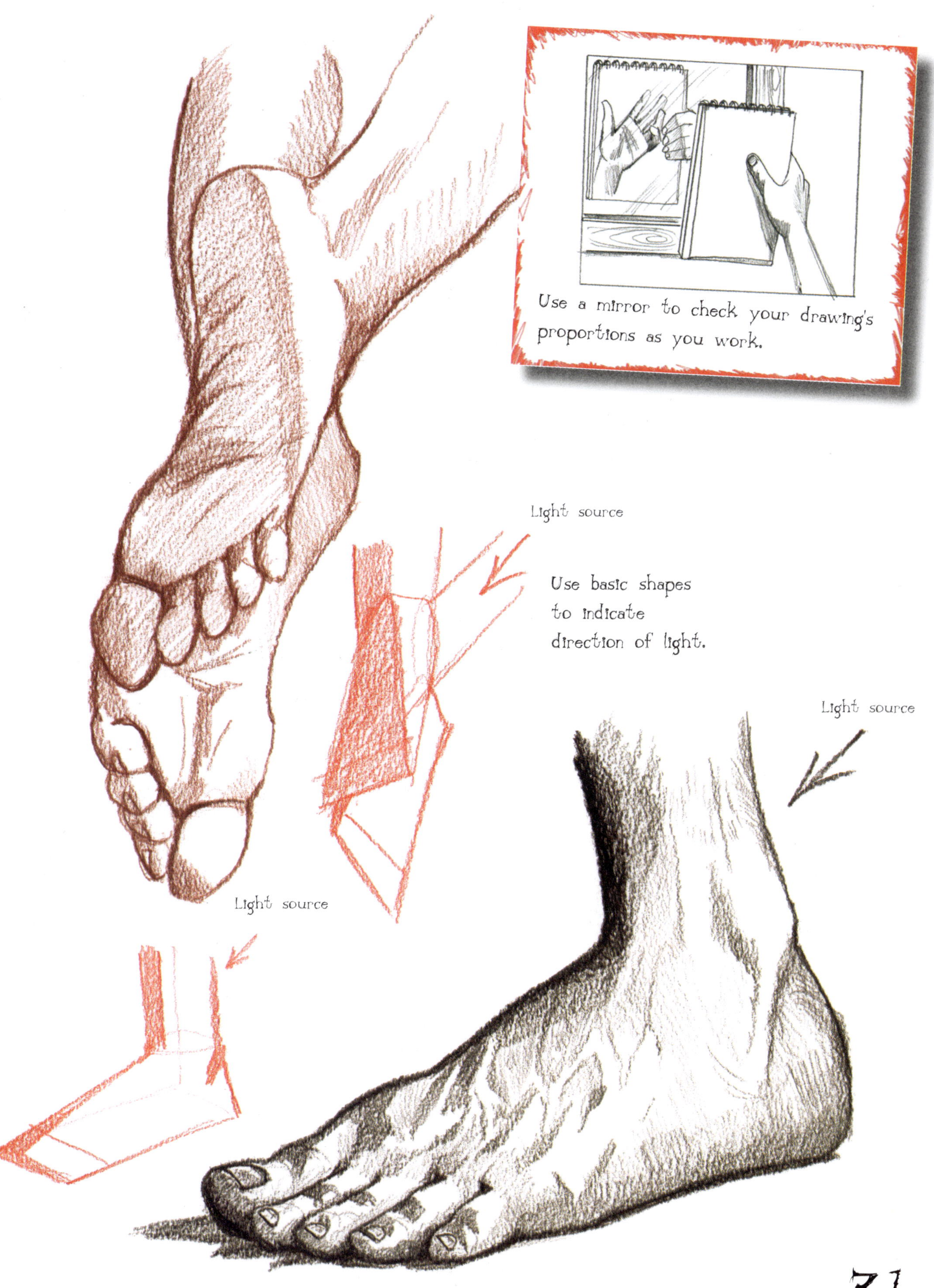

Use a mirror to check your drawing's proportions as you work.

Light source

Use basic shapes
to indicate
direction of light.

Light source

Light source

Glossary

Collagen   A protein in the body that keeps skin strong.

Cross-hatching   The use of criss-crossed lines to indicate dense shade in a drawing.

Hatching   The use of parallel lines to indicate light shade in a drawing.

Light source   The direction from which the light seems to come in a drawing.

Perspective   A method of drawing in which near objects are shown larger than faraway objects to give an impression of depth.

Proportion   The correct relationship of scale between each part of the drawing.

Silhouette   A drawing that shows only a flat dark shape, like a shadow.

Index